~~Baby~~ Parent Dedication

God's Seed Placed in Your Hand

Learning How to Step into Your Calling as Your Child's Spiritual Leader and Teacher

Alicia White

Parent Dedication
Copyright © 2019 by Alicia White
Published by Chosen Stones Ministries
Email: info@ChosenStones.org
Web: www.chosenstones.org

Contents

Introduction

Several months ago, I was reading an article that was going around social media. A mother was sharing an experience she had with her child's baby dedication in her church.

Her Pastor gave her, and I am assuming her husband, a jar full of pennies. He goes on to explain that there were 936 pennies in the jar, a penny for every week you will raise your child. He instructed the parents to take out a penny every Sunday when they come home from church. With each week, he explained, the heavy weighty jar would get lighter and lighter. You will be reminded, he said, week after week, of the amount of time you have left to raise your children up in the Lord.

The mother then added her own thoughts as to what happened week after week. They never removed the pennies. The jar just sat on a desk as a reminder. To remove the pennies, would only make the weight of the jar heavier within their heart.

This story hit home with me – a mother of four kids, a 21-year-old, a 17- year-old, a 16-year-old, and a 9-year-old; I understand very well what it means to feel the weight of the years gone by. There is a lot I wish I would have done, many things I am glad I did, and some things I wish I wouldn't have done. But the reality is, I can't get one week back. Time stays still for no one. As a mother of an infant, I remember when I wish it would go faster, but now looking back, I wouldn't have traded those moments for anything in the world.

As I pondered the experience this mother was sharing, I realized that baby dedications were not really about the babies at all. In time, they would make their own decision whether or not they would dedicate their lives to Jesus. Baby dedications are really ***parent dedications***. They are a public ceremony as such, to commission the parents to train up a child in the way they should go – that way being Jesus.

The dedication is a charge for them to take up their God-given calling as the spiritual leader and teacher of their child. It is essentially a moment the Pastor looks the parents in the eye and says, "Tag you're it!" At that moment, He may look at the congregation, elders, and leaders of the church and charge them with being a helpmate to the parents. But the weight of the responsibility is placed in the parent's hand, and they are sent off to do the job at hand with maybe a bottle of anointing oil and a child's Bible. Little or no instructions are ever given from the pulpit, and the church has failed to disciple and equip parents in any other way. Family ministry of any kind is rarely, if not ever, modeled in the house of God. The majority of the parents in the body today are a generation or two out from any kind of family ministry model in the home or church. They do not have a clue how to teach their children spiritual things. They feel ill-equipped, and as a result, they have given up their calling into the hands of children's ministry leader and teachers.

This book was created to be a vision casting book for parents. It gives parents Biblical and prophetic insight into their number one calling of life – parenting. He helps them to have the courage to take back the baton, and become the spiritual teacher of their children. And it begins to equip them with strategies of spiritual parenting, which in days ahead, will keep them on target.

It is a spiritual parenting book that Pastors and leaders can place into the hands of new parents at the time of baby dedications or in the hands of any and all parents of the church. It is a great gift for expecting parents as well. It is meant to be a quick read, filled with deep and prophetic truths, to initially equip the parents of the body.

Parent Dedication

Chapter 1

God Choose You

"And these words which I command you today shall be in your heart. You shall teach them diligently to your children, and shall talk of them when you sit in your house, when you walk by the way, when you lie down, and when you rise up. You shall bind them as a sign on your hand, and they shall be as frontlets between your eyes. You shall write them on the doorposts of your house and on your gates." (Deuteronomy 6:6-9).

Tag you're it! God has chosen you! He has not chosen your church, the children's ministry of your church, your Pastor, nor your parents, or friends. He has chosen *you* to spiritually teach your child. Or should I say... *His* child. This can be a very weighty burden on any shoulder of a parent. But whom He has chosen, He will anoint. When your child cried their first cry that echoed through the space of time from earth to heaven, the Holy Spirit responded and poured out His anointing from heaven to earth. An exchange happened that day. God gave up His seed, in exchange for a bit more of His kingdom to come to earth. Welcome to the greatest calling you will ever have in life.

I remember when my third child was an infant. Three is a difficult number. The children suddenly outnumber the adults. A scary thought. I was overwhelmed in so many ways. I had found my way back to Jesus years prior after walking away for eight years. I was falling madly in love with Him. For the first time I was walking in a deep relationship with Him, looking forward to awakening every day to being with Him. But the age between my second and third child was only fifteen months a part. I had my hands full for sure.

I begin to struggle to find time with the Lord. Suddenly my life was all about diapers, spit up, rocking, and entertaining children. I missed Him. One day I began to cry out and tell Him how much I desired to be with Him, when suddenly His voice became so clear to me. He said, "Alicia, look into the eyes of your children. Did you not know that they are My glory manifested? They are the closest tangible manifestation to the very purest part of My presence. I have been with you this whole time."

It was a light bulb moment. In that moment I realized what a privilege I had in holding my children, rocking my children, playing with my children, loving my children; I was pouring out my life and dwelling with the Father the whole time. A part of heaven, a part of God, was in my arms. What would be my response? I realized for the first time this was more than having a family or raising children, this was a calling. An assignment from heaven. He chose me to nurture a part of Himself, what a precious gift!

Teach Them to Love the Lord

So, what is your assignment/calling from heaven as a parent? In Deuteronomy 6:6 God says, "These words which I command you today." What are those words of God?

"Hear, O Israel: The LORD our God, the LORD is one! You shall love the LORD your God with all your heart, with all your soul, and with all your strength." (Deuteronomy 6:4-5).

And in case you needed it in a New Testament reference, here is how Jesus said it, *"You shall love the LORD your God with all your heart, with all your soul, and with all your mind. This is the first and greatest commandment. And the second is like it: You shall love your neighbor as yourself." (Matthew 22:37-39).*

Our assignment as the caregiver of God's seed sent from heaven is to teach them how to love God and people. It is not to give them our religion or command them to love Jesus. It is to show them how to love Jesus with all they are; relationship not religion. Out of that overflow they will love others and the full manifestation of everything God has placed in them as a seed, will come to pass. His glory sent from heaven to earth in your child will bring forth fruit. He has chosen you, come, arise to the calling set before you.

His Perfect Timing

I want you to know God has chosen you to be the parent of your child for such a time as this. And He has chosen your child to be your son or daughter for such a time as this. Think about that for a moment. God reached down into humanity's timeline and said - now is the time for you. He knows the end from the beginning. He could have chosen you or your kids to be born in the 1800's, 20's, or 50's, but He chose you to be a family for the now. This is the time He has called you to be a parent, and this is the time He has called your child to be a child of God. God is intentional in everything He does. Nothing is by accident or happenchance. There is a reason and a purpose in all things for those who are called by His name. A precious seed God planted in a womb was brought to the surface of the earth. The child you hold in your arms was prepared for the now. There is something you and your child can only do in this moment of time, your lifetime, which no one else has been assigned to do. You are not just a speck of sand on the shore of time, you have been anointed for this.

The world we live in today is violent. You can almost tangibly feel the warfare between darkness and light. Prophecy is being fulfilled almost daily and there is no doubt Jesus' second coming is soon. So why now? Why has God chosen you and your child for this day and hour?

Behold, I will send you Elijah the prophet before the coming of the great and dreadful day of the LORD. And he will turn the hearts of the fathers to the children, and the hearts of the children to their fathers, lest I come and strike the earth with a curse." (Malachi 4:5-6)

I want to stay right here for a moment and share what I believe is a prophetic assignment for families in this day and hour. These are the last words spoken right before the four hundred years of silence and Jesus' first coming, and I believe they are the prophetic words for His church today to prepare His Bride for the second coming of Christ. Families are more separated today than ever before. We go to church and separate, and we come home and separate. The family altar is almost nonexistent. This is destroying the church from the inside out. Broken families have created broken churches.

Family was the very first entity God created and the very way in which He chose to multiply His glory on this earth. Family is the lens God created to view the gospel and relationship between humanity and deity. As the family is destroyed, it prevents the gospel from being received and God's glory from covering the earth. It has been and will always be Satan's target in the battle of the Kingdoms. This is why you see the anti-Christ spirit going after the family so much in the homosexual agenda, abortion, and transgender agenda, pornography addiction, and drug and alcohol abuse.

But in the midst of all this darkness God gives us this word. *Now* is time to turn the hearts of families back to each other and to God. He is preparing His Bride from the inside out and you get to be part of that. Now is your time. Now is your assignment and calling. I believe your family is called to for such a time as this.

He Trusts You

And if He has chosen you, He trusts you. The idea of raising a
child who is completely dependent upon you to teach them
everything they need to know to love the Lord and people, is
overwhelming to say the least. From the time your baby breathed
their first breath of earthly oxygen, they have looked to you for
everything. They immediately and without question trusted you,
and so does your heavenly Father. He has given you His most
precious gift, His seed. You are an entrusted with not just a son or
daughter, but a child of God Himself. His DNA. The one He knew
before you ever imagined them within your arms.

*"For You formed my inward parts; You covered me in my mother's
womb. I will praise You, for I am fearfully and wonderfully made;
Marvelous are Your works, And that my soul knows very well. My
frame was not hidden from You, when I was made in secret, And
skillfully wrought in the lowest parts of the earth. Your eyes saw
my substance, being yet unformed. And in Your book they all were
written, the days fashioned for me, when as yet there were none
of them. And in Your book they all were written, the days
fashioned for me, when as yet there were none of them." (Psalm
139:13-16).*

I believe somehow, far beyond our mind to imagine, God
sovereignly knows the plans and purposes He has for each one of
us before we were even formed in our mother's womb. He knew
your children; He knew exactly the right time for them to be
birthed on earth and with whom He could entrust to love them,
nurture them, and prepare them to manifest the plans of God on
this earth. He trusts you!

Kingdom, Family, Purpose

God's heart has always been about family. God is not just a creator, He is a Father. He is God, He is Father; completely in control of His family.

Then God said, "Let Us make man in Our image, according to Our likeness; let them have dominion over the fish of the sea, over the birds of the air, and over the cattle, over all the earth and over every creeping thing that creeps on the earth." (Genesis 1:26).

God had family in mind when he created humanity. We are just not humans taking up space on this earth, but citizens of the Kingdom of Heaven and children of the King. Our King breathed into us His DNA and handed us His scepter of righteousness, justice, and power through the Holy Spirit, that we may use it to subdue the earth and create heaven on earth. Jesus said to pray this, *"Your kingdom come, Your will be done, on earth as it is in heaven."* (Matthew 6:10). This prayer can only happen through me, you, and His seed. If I were to narrow God's purpose for our life, our children's lives, and this earth, down to one thing, it would be this:

God's purpose is to have a family who acts like their heavenly Father and walks in a manifested state of "thy kingdom come thy will be done" until all the earth mirrors that of heaven. Family was the establishment and paradigm God created on earth to make a family of sons and daughters who looked like and acted like the King, consequently creating a culture and society on earth that looked like and acted like the Kingdom of Heaven.

This was the original purpose of the garden. He took heaven and transposed it to earth and then created His children to walk out the purpose of heaven on earth.

The Perfect Parent

A daddy full of eternal, everlasting, and unconditional love for His children awaits a mother and father in the flesh who He can live through. He is the only perfect parent. We cannot and will never be a perfect parent. But He awaits the opportunity He can live through us.

This is the true miracle of spiritual parenting; a yielded heart ready to grab hold of the Father's love and purposes for our children. A partnership with the perfected Father will always yield the highest results. He loves them more than you do. That's hard to imagine isn't? But the truth is we can't love them like He can. Our love does have limits as much as we would like to think it doesn't for our children. But their heavenly Father, the one who knew them before we did, desires to love them through us.

You are the voice of the Father to your children. Yes, they can absolutely hear from God themselves as they begin to walk in their own relationship with Him, but you are the first voice of the Father they will hear. Their encounter will influence how they see the Father. You are the natural manifestation of a supernatural God. Not perfected in the flesh, but an unperfected reflection of the one who is perfect. This is why it is so important you hear from God when it comes to parenting. We will talk about this concept further in the book, but for now I want you to know, you can't and will never be a perfect parent. Give yourself room to make mistakes. God's grace will do what you can't.

The Abraham Moment

Spiritual parenting is a calling and a ministry. It is the single most important calling you will ever have in your life. You are taking part in shaping this earth, culture, and life as we know it. Parenting is all about being a part of something greater than yourself. How you raise your children, shape and cultivate the seed God has given you, will directly affect not only you, them, but the generations to come.

I love the story that unfolds in Genesis 18:17-19. It really gives us a bird's eye view into God's purpose for us as parents, and the weight of the calling set before us.

The scene unfolds as a conversation God has concerning Abraham right before He declares His judgment on Sodom and Gomorrah. The culture of which Abraham lived in was wicked, sexually perverse, self-centered, and indulging. Does that sound familiar to you? God's timing of judgement on the culture in Genesis was about to be poured out, but before doing so, He wanted to make sure that He found the one family who He could use once again to assure His kingdom could continue to advance on this earth. This story sounds a lot like the Malachi prophecy doesn't it?

The passage goes like this, *"And the LORD said, 'Shall I hide from Abraham what I am doing, since Abraham shall surely become a great and mighty nation, and all the nations of the earth shall be blessed in him? For I have known him, in order that he may command his children and his household after him, that they keep the way of the LORD, to do righteousness and justice, that the LORD may bring to Abraham what He has spoken to him'." (Genesis 18:17-19).*

Abraham was not chosen by God to be the Father of the nations because He was a great anointed man who could do signs and wonders. No, Abraham was chosen by God because He was a Godly daddy who chose to use his seed and his family, to influence the earth with the principals and characteristics of the Kingdom of Heaven. God needed a family for such a time as that, and He found one in Abraham.

I believe we are living in a time and season much like Abraham was living in. Our Sodom and Gomorrah is all around us. God's judgment is not far away.

God is speaking to those mothers and fathers who have an ear to hear what the spirit of the Lord is saying; this is our Abraham moment. The greatest act of worship we could ever give to God is to give our children to Him. To lay them at the altar and say, "Whatever it looks like God, they are yours, do with them as you please."

I still remember the moment I did that with our oldest child. I don't talk about it much because it comes with strange circumstances, but here it goes. Samuel, our now twenty-one-year-old, was a toddler. He was potty training. After he had his first bowel movement in the toilet, he freaked out. It scared him I guess to see something like that come out of him. Now that I am thinking of it, I guess it could freak anyone out that doesn't understand what is happening. He developed a fear of having a bowel movement. Now that may not sound like much, but imagine having a toddler who would do just about anything to hold in his poop. He would cry and freak out when he couldn't hold it in any longer, and would sometimes go in his pants. We couldn't take him anywhere for fear of an episode. We knew it could eventually turn into a very serious physical condition with complications if we didn't get it under control.

Now let me give you a bit of the back story. I was a first-time mom, who had walked away from the Lord for eight years. I had already battled through colic that was so bad he had to have hernia repair surgery at one years old from crying so hard. I was exhausted and ready to throw in the towel at this point, and that place of surrender was exactly where God wanted me to be. I remember the day I took him to the altar. Except it wasn't a stone altar - it was a porcelain toilet! I was begging him to relax and let the poop come out. He was crying and I was crying. In that moment of desperation, I said out loud to God, "God, if you deliver my son from this fear and allow Him to poop, I will give him to you all the days of his life." Now, those are not the most beautiful words of surrender you may have ever heard, and certainly not the most beautiful scene to imagine, but that day was my Abraham moment. He went to the bathroom and from that day on he never had an issue with it.

My end of the promise to the Lord came into fulfillment only after my second miscarriage several years later. I found my way back to Jesus. From that day on, I began to step into my calling and began to give Samuel over to the Lord. And just so I can place a period into the end of this story. Samuel's birth name given to him was actually named Tristan. But when he was seven, we heard God speak to us as parents that we named him Tristan, but God had named him Samuel.

I still remember it so clearly. We were leaders at our church during a revival service. Samuel was helping place the drop cloth over people as they fell out in the spirit. One of the women attending the conference came over to me and said, "Your son is anointed with the spirit of Samuel. He will be a priest and prophet to his generation." I immediately felt my spirit jolt. I knew God was speaking. I kept it to myself for weeks and begin to pray. I heard the Lord during that time speak the words, "You have named him Tristan, but I have named him Samuel." I asked the Lord to speak to Jason, my husband, separately to confirm He was asking us to change His name. After several days, I felt the Lord prompt me to speak to Jason about it. Jason interrupted me as I began and said the Lord had spoken to him last week about changing his name as well. It was confirmed.

So, on his eighth birthday, the day of new beginnings, Tristan was watered baptized. Our second Abraham moment. He went down as Tristan and came up as Samuel. We had his name officially changed several years later. I could never imagine the words I prayed over "Tristan" in that bathroom, years before I knew God would ask us to change his name to Samuel, would be the very words Hannah spoke over Samuel in 1 Samuel 1:28, *"Now I am giving him to the LORD, and he will belong to the LORD his whole life." (NLT2).*

Today, Samuel is at Christ for the Nations studying ministry. He is a world changer and was birthed to be a Priest and Prophet to his generation. I often wonder what would have become of His life had I not surrendered that day in the bathroom. Would I have poured into Him Jesus; taught him how to love Jesus and people? Would I have seen the purposes God placed in our son before He was in my womb ever come to pass?

God is seeking those who will answer the call to raise their children to do righteousness and justice in this Sodom and Gomorrah time and season. He still desires to use families to fulfill His greatest call and purposes on this earth; to be His inheritance and to expand His kingdom on Earth. Abraham made the choice to surrender to his greatest call; his parenting was intentional and purpose-driven to the point he was willing to offer up His only son as a sacrifice to the Lord in an act of obedience. Are you ready to be that kind of parent who is willing to give your children completely and freely over to God for Him to do as He pleases? Are you ready to be a family for God's Kingdom who God can trust to influence and expand heaven on earth?

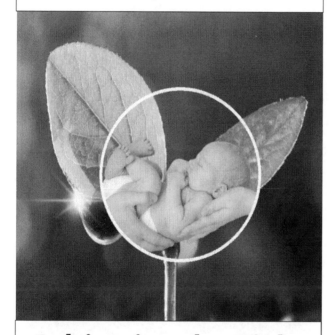

Chapter 2

Cultivating the Right Atmosphere

The Seed Sent from Heaven

Often in scripture the Lord will use seed as an analogy, sometimes meaning His Word and oftentimes meaning, His children. I believe one is not absent from the other.

Jesus was sent as the Word of God made flesh, both a seed and a word from heaven. I believe our children are as well.

Your child is a word sent from heaven, a seed planted on earth. Of course, not the perfect and unfaultable word of God Jesus was – but a word from God, full of potential, promise, and fruit just ready to be planted, nurtured, and cultivated into a beautiful manifestation of heaven on earth.

We already talked about how God knew each one of us before we were even conceived. Could it be we were His word, life ready to be spoken, seed ready to be placed in a womb, both physically and spiritually? God was just waiting on the right atmosphere that would be conducive to bringing forth the life. Seed needs the right conditions in order to bring out its full potential. Have you ever seen a tree that was potted in a small house pot? It never grows to be twelve feet tall because it doesn't live in the right atmosphere. Atmosphere means everything to a seed. A good seed planted in the wrong atmosphere will not produce fruit but die, never reaching its full potential.

Now, I have to admit I do not have a green thumb whatsoever. You give me a plant and it will be dead in a month. But I think I might be slightly better at cultivating spiritual seeds, thank God! I do know some basics of seed planting that perhaps we all can draw from for spiritual application.

So, let's find out what atmosphere it is going to take for your seed to produce fruit.

Right Container

If you are going to plant a seed, you have to first determine what you are going to plant it in. The container has to reflect the maturity expected to happen. What will that seed look like when maturity comes full circle?

Our goal is to raise holy and righteous children who live their life to serve, love, and obey Christ. With that in mind let's talk about the container of our children for a minute. The container of our seed is our home. Our home will be the place we plant God's seed to grow and mature. It is not to be the church, it is not the school, it is not daycare; it is our home.

Is your home prepared to hold the potential of God's seed? I am going to come out of the gate on this one not mixing words. I am telling your right now many containers in the body of Christ are not ready for God's glory. If righteousness and holiness is what is inside of your children, you must make sure your container, your home, is cultivating that same kind of atmosphere. What kind of things does Jesus find in your home? What movies do you watch, what books do you read, what entertains you?

When, according to many statics, 85% of our men in our Christian homes struggle with pornography —our containers have a sexual crisis. Sexual perversion of all kinds has contaminated our homes. This isn't just with pornography, but with infidelity and sexual lust of all kinds.

"Being filled with all unrighteousness, sexual immorality, wickedness, covetousness, maliciousness; full of envy, murder, strife, deceit, evil-mindedness; they are whisperers, backbiters, haters of God, violent, proud, boasters, inventors of evil things, disobedient to parents, undiscerning, untrustworthy, unloving, unforgiving, unmerciful; who, knowing the righteous judgment of God, that those who practice such things are deserving of death,

21

not only do the same but also approve of those who practice them." (Romans 1:29-32).

Many of our homes are not filled with righteousness and holiness and this is affecting our word sent from heaven. If we want the fruit of the glory of God to manifest in your children, it starts with the container. One of the biggest struggles I see within today's families is the compromise found with what entertains our eyes. The door to our souls. Movies like Harry Potter, Twilight, demonic driven entertainment that emphases the underworld and darkness, and the sexual lust of the flesh, has saturated worldly entertainment today. We can't get away from it, but we can control how much of it fills our container.

"There shall not be found among you anyone who makes his son or his daughter pass through the fire, or one who practices witchcraft, or a soothsayer, or one who interprets omens, or a sorcerer, or one who conjures spells, or a medium, or a spiritist, or one who calls up the dead. For all who do these things are an abomination to the LORD, and because of these abominations the LORD your God drives them out from before you." (Deuteronomy 18:10-12).

If these things are sin in God's eyes, why do we think it is ok to be entertained by them? We are coming into agreement with them, even if we are not engaging in it physically. Here is how I handle anything I choose to do in my home, or even outside of my home. If I cannot offer up a seat beside me and invite Jesus Christ to join me in what I am doing, I shouldn't be doing it. This is what we should be teaching our children as well.

One of the biggest issues I see within many parents of the body right now, is alcohol drinking. In Judges 13:4-5, the Lord instructs the mother of Sampson to not drink while she was pregnant with Sampson, for He was called from the womb to be a Nazarite.

God was preparing the container to hold the potential of the seed. What his mother did in the natural, directly affected what her son would accomplish in the supernatural. That is powerful and worth reading again! Nowhere in scripture does it tell us it is a sin to drink, but it does say it is to get drunk (Galatians 5:21).

Did you know that children who have parents who drink are 3x more likely to abuse alcohol as teenagers? That doesn't say if their parents get drunk, it simply means if they see their parents drink at all.

"But if you cause one of these little ones who trusts in me to fall into sin, it would be better for you to have a large millstone tied around your neck and be drowned in the depths of the sea." *(Matthew 18:6).*

Because I have seen such destruction of families from alcohol, I want to give you a few more scriptures and Biblical principles on this subject to meditate on.

- Deuteronomy 29:6 tells us that God never allowed any of His children that were permitted to come into the Promised Land, to drink wine or similar drink the whole entire time in the wilderness.
- Proverbs 20:1 *"Wine is a mocker, Strong drink is a brawler, and whoever is led astray by it is not wise."*
- Did you know that the priests were not allow to drink alcohol when going into the temple (Leviticus 10:8)? This is important for us to know because according to 1 Corinthians 3:16, we are the New Testament temple, and according to 1 Peter 2:9, we are also the New Testament Priest.

- According to Luke 1:15 John the Baptist was forbidden to drink alcohol at any time.

Drinking a glass of wine will not send you to hell, but I believe it may become a stumbling block for you and your children's relationship with Jesus. Why do we expect or settle for anything less than the higher calling for us and our seed?

Keep the container prepared to handle all the glory of God locked up within God's seed.

Right Soil

Soil is what will provide the nutrient your seed will need to grow. Jesus said, *"Man does not live by bread alone, but on every word that precedes out of the mouth of God." (Matthew 4:4).* Your word sent from heaven, your child, needs the Word sent from heaven, in order to thrive. They need to be planted deep within the soil of the Word of God. If we are going to teach them how to love God, they must know who God is.

Your container, your house, must be filled with the Word of God. Deuteronomy 6:6-9 again says, *You shall teach them diligently to your children, and shall talk of them when you sit in your house, when you walk by the way, when you lie down, and when you rise up. You shall bind them as a sign on your hand, and they shall be as frontlets between your eyes. You shall write them on the doorposts of your house and on your gates.* God's word must be a constant conversation in your home. Your children need to have a Biblical worldview of all that life has to offer. If they don't, they will take on the world's view of their life. Whichever lens they look through will become how they make life decisions that will shape who they will become.

"For the word of God is living and powerful, and sharper than any two-edged sword, piercing even to the division of soul and spirit,

and of joints and marrow, and is a discerner of the thoughts and intents of the heart." (Hebrews 4:12).

The word of God has the capacity to get down deep inside your seed and pull out anything that hinders God's glory in them. As a family, I encourage you to read the Word of God together. I have some excellent devotionals, but there are countless others on the market to use.

But just as important as the written Word of God is to developing good soil, the testimony of God in your family's life cultivates the soil as well.

"And they overcame him by the blood of the Lamb and by the word of their testimony." (Revelation 12:11).

The testimony of Christ in a persons' life not only brings faith to the soil of their own seed, but when shared, saturates the soil of others with faith as well. I love the story found in Joshua 4. The children of God are finally getting to cross over the Jordon into the Promised Land. As the priest's garments hit the water, God suddenly parts the water. While they are still standing in the middle of the Jordan, holding the ark, God commands them to do this act of worship, "Take for yourselves twelve stones from here, out of the midst of the Jordan, from the place where the priests' feet stood firm. You shall carry them over with you and leave them in the lodging place where you lodge tonight." (Joshua 4:3) Then God goes on to say why He wants them to do this prophetic act, "That this may be a sign among you when your children ask in time to come, saying, 'What do these stones mean to you?' Then you shall answer them that the waters of the Jordan were cut off before the ark of the covenant of the LORD; when it crossed over the Jordan, the waters of the Jordan were cut off. And these stones shall be for a memorial to the children of Israel forever." (Joshua 4:6-7.) It was SO important to God that they commemorate this that the priests were STILL standing there and *not instructed to cross, until it was done! WOW. This gets me. We should be intentional to remember what God has done.* God was ensuring that one generation to the next would know His ways, see Him manifested on earth, and prepare their soil to bring forth fruit.

Within a book I created for parents called, *Stone Moments*, I included a prophetic act of family worship connected to this story in Joshua. My family and I actually do this prophetic act every New Year's Eve. We ask each member of the family to write down all God did for them that year and write down all they want God to do for the next year. We gather together and share our "stones." Every year has been collected and put in a box. One day we will get them out and read them and see what all God has done through our family.

It is important that you share with your child your testimony. How God has worked in your life. This prepares the soil of faith for them to believe in their own life.

Water and Light

All seeds in order to grow, need water and light. Along with the food of the soil, it is what gives them the power and energy to grow. A seed without water and light will rot, wither away, and die, never to see its potential. Your seed needs the power and presence of the Holy Spirit in their lives.

"For our gospel did not come to you in word only, but also in power." (1 Thessalonians 1:5)

I am going to say something here that may shock some, especially those in a religious mindset. The written Word of God alone is not good enough to bring your seed into their full potential. A seed with good rich soil will never grow, and die right where it is, without water and light. This is why religion never produces God's glory. If God's Word alone was enough, God would have never had to send his Word, manifested in the flesh, to the cross for the redemption and reconciliation of mankind. It was the power of the Holy Spirit that raised Jesus from the dead (water), and the presence of the Word, made flesh through Jesus (light), which brought life and fruit to humanity. Today, we don't have Jesus physically, but He has not left us alone, but sent His Holy Spirit to dwell in us (John 15:16).

It is the truth of God's Word MIXED with power and presence of the sprit in your child that will cause their seed to mature. Your child needs to know about the Holy Spirit, His works, His gifts, and be filled to overflowing.

"On the last day, that great day of the feast, Jesus stood and cried out, saying, "If anyone thirsts, let him come to Me and drink. He who believes in Me, as the Scripture has said, out of his heart will flow rivers of living water." (John 7:37-38)

Your seed needs water; the water of the Holy Spirit. In fact, I think we have been so guilty of planting children of God in contaminated containers with good soil and then expecting them to grow? Children naturally are thirsty for the water, all we need to do is bring them to the power of the Holy Spirit and let Him do the work. In fact, I do not believe they can ever carry the nature and character of Christ without the power of the Spirit. We can't expect them to manifest the fruits of the Spirit without drinking from the Spirit.

Here is what I have learned from years of ministering to families and kids. A hunger for the Word of God can only be increased in a person's life when they have experienced the Word made alive; the light of Jesus' presence. Put a plant in the dark and see how long it lives.

I think some of my personal problems with growing house plants have been that, up until recently, most of my windows have been covered up by couches, dressers, furniture of some kind, so I have not been able to place a plant by the window and let the light shine on it. I actually just rearranged most of my windows to make them clear of furniture.

Plants long for light. In fact, most of them grow towards the light. Isn't that what you want? Your children to grow towards the light of His presence?

"I am the light of the world. He who follows Me shall not walk in darkness, but have the light of life." (John 8:12).

It is the presence of Jesus that gives us light to live and destroys all darkness.

"Oh, taste and see that the LORD is good; blessed is the man who trusts in Him!" (Psalm 34:8).

God's presence is experiential. It needs to be experienced. Have you ever thought about how you could explain or teach a blind person about light? It would be very difficult. Light is meant to be experienced. This is why people who have not been in the Presence of God do not understand the response of someone who has. The more you experience the very manifestation of His Presence, the more you want to.

Introduce your children to His presence and watch them start to grow towards it. Take them to revival services and make sure your church home is filled and active in the Spirit of God.

Shifting Atmospheres

I have cultivated an atmosphere of light in my home. In fact, I believe it is one of my jobs as the mother of my home. Women carry a natural and spiritual womb to shift atmospheres. In fact, just by looking at the spelling of woman itself, you could derive the words womb and man. Every living soul must come through the womb of a woman. A womb is an atmosphere conducive for a seed to grow. Women have a natural womb that I believe is a manifestation of the spiritual womb.

I shift atmospheres in my home in many different ways, but prayer and worship are priority. God's presence is always manifested where there is communion with Him and worship for Him. I have made it my goal to bring an atmosphere of worship in my home by constantly playing worship music. It's rare to walk into my home and not hear it. In fact, all of our children play it throughout the night in their room.

I open the windows of heaven and invite the presence of Jesus, His light into our home. Make worship a lifestyle. Let your children, even as infants, see you worship and pray. Your family, your kids, will begin to recognize the reality of Jesus, His love, His nature in the home. It will shift the mood and fill your home with His light.

I want to share a really cool exercise that my son just experienced in a young adult camp he went to several summers ago with Lance Wallnau. A couple that was there who walk out their faith in their homes with their kids, taught the camp what they do in their home to shift the atmosphere. You know, when things get crazy in your home and if feels more dark than light? This is a good time to do this prophetic exercise. They first ask everyone in the room to stop and be still and feel the atmosphere in the room. Even toddlers can sense atmosphere, so don't hesitate to ask them what they feel in a language they would understand. What emotions are you feeling, what sounds can you hear still ringing in your ear? Then have everyone raise their hands and slowly count down 3, 2, and 1. Slowly and calmly speak the word Love, or peace, or Joy. Have everyone participate. Repeat the counting down and spoken word three times, or as many times as it takes to shift the atmosphere. This is what they called becoming an architect of atmosphere.

That is what we are as parents. We are the architects, following the master architect's plans, to create and environment conducive for God's seed to reach its full potential.

Chapter 3

Welcome to the Front Lines

Battle of the Kingdoms

Since the time of Adam and Eve's sin, Satan has waged war for the soul of humanity. He is after God's seed and desires to increase His kingdom of darkness through one generation to the next.

But this does not surprise God. In fact, He set up a plan right there in Genesis to war against the Kingdom of Darkness. God said to Satan in the garden, *"And I will put enmity between you and the woman, and between your seed and her Seed; He shall bruise your head, and you shall bruise His heel." (Genesis 3:15).* God sent His only son, His seed, through a family on earth, to defeat Satan and His Kingdom.

"And from the days of John the Baptist until now the kingdom of heaven suffers violence, and the violent take it by force." (Matthew 11:12).

The battle of the Kingdoms is still raging today. And God's plan is still in place; to use the seed of God to destroy the works of the devil. Yes, Jesus made a way at the cross for our victory, but the battle is still guaranteed. Satan is still roaming the earth to steal, kill, and destroy the family of God one seed at a time. Like it or not, as a parent, you just engaged in that war with a new assignment. You no longer can sit back and watch from the side lines. You, my friend, are on the front lines.

Your Weapon

"Behold, children are a heritage from the LORD; the fruit of the womb is a reward. Like arrows in the hand of a warrior, so are the children of one's youth. Happy is the man who has his quiver full of them; they shall not be ashamed, But shall speak with their enemies in the gate." (Psalm 127:3-6).

Those on the front lines between the kingdom of darkness and kingdom of light are not without a weapon. God's choice for the battle is His seed, your arrows. He has prepared and equipped you, but it is up to you to engage in this battle. If you do not, the consequences may be the destruction of your seed into the hands of the enemy.

This may sound very mellow-dramatic to you as a parent, especially if you are a new parent with an infant. Here I am talking to you about warfare and somehow your child is a weapon. Your perspective is far from war, but one with sweet smiles, cuddle times, baby smells, and cues. You're looking forward to them talking, crawling, and walking. You can't wait for the family vacations and soccer games.

All those things you no doubt will experience, and I pray you take it all in and enjoy it. But this book was not written out of a desire to make parenting a bed of roses. It is a book about parent's dedication to their children's spiritual life and maturity. To ignore that the spiritual realm has two kingdoms warring against each other for the soul of your child, would be irresponsible of me and not truth imparted. I am certain if you are a parent with a teenager or know of one who is, the perspective is a lot closer to the war I am describing than not.

I also want you to know that if your child is an infant, do not think it to be long before you have to deal with spiritual warfare. Remember they tried to kill Jesus as an infant, and the Kingdom of Darkness did manage to kill many children under two during that time. Satan is no respecter of person or age.

Often, without even our awareness, Satan is in the background trying to divert God's seed placed in our hands. Many times, he is more aware of the potential placed in our children than we are. I look back on my own children. I have already talked to you about Samuel. The one thing I did not share, is that he was a miracle baby from the beginning. When I was eight months pregnant with him I begin to go into labor. He was still small – five pounds – so they tried to stop labor. After about sixteen hours, they realized there was no stopping it, and thank God! They did not realize until after he was delivered, that my placenta had torn and he was in distress, having swallowed a lot of blood. Knowing what I have already told you about him, there is no question this was an attack trying to hinder the promises of God locked up in him before he was even born. He was a weapon of God created for spiritual warfare. I wasn't even walking with the Lord at the time, but God still protected him.

Our battle for the life of our children did not stop at Samuel. We had two miscarriages after him. After the second miscarriage, I gave my life back to Jesus. I got pregnant again – only to get very sick with the flu and pneumonia. I was running a 104 temperature, and during an early ultrasound, they told me the cells were already breaking up and I was in the middle of my third miscarriage. Something – the Holy Spirit (and faith, no doubt), rose up in me that day, and I said to the doctor, "I respect your opinion but the Great Physician will have the last word." Jason, my husband, called the church, and one of the Pastors came over and prayed with us. The next week I had another ultrasound, due to not having any miscarriage symptoms... and the pregnancy was viable.

This was a testimony of faith that brought salvation to my husband, and so we several months later got water baptized together. Our battle for our seed, for God's weapon of choice, was not over yet though. Shortly after our water baptism and my husband's salvation, we had our fifth month ultrasound. The technician placed us in a room afterwards and the doctor came in looking very somber. He told us our daughter had a kidney disease. Her chances of living were fifty percent or less, and if she did live, she would have to have a kidney transplant. We walked out devastated. The bad news didn't stop there. Jason also got laid off that same week which happened to be Father's Day weekend. Talk about baptism by fire!

The church gathered around us and prayed until I gave birth to her four months later. Our second miracle baby was born with only one functioning kidney, but healthy otherwise. It turns out, they misdiagnosed her, and although she did have a kidney disease, it was not as bad as they thought. We named her Faithanna. She is graduating high school this year with a full year of college already under her belt. She plans on becoming a nurse practitioner and using her degree on the mission field.

Ok, are you ready for our third miracle arrow that the enemy tried to abort from this world? Our Hope. Faithanna was only eight months old when I got pregnant with Hope. It was not planned, especially since my husband was laid off. But of course, we were ready to receive another child into the world we could share God's love with. Early in my pregnancy, I began to have miscarriage symptoms. It was a holiday weekend, and the doctor over the phone, pretty much told to let things happen naturally. But three days later, although bleeding and cramping, I still felt pregnant. I called and demanded they give me an ultrasound. They confirmed I was a having a miscarriage, but of twins. I had one viable seed still with a heartbeat in the womb! Although I hemorrhaged going to labor with her, Hope was born right after Christmas. The best Christmas present ever! Hope is working hard in High School, loves Jesus, and is called to be hope to the hopeless! A mighty arrow for the Lord!

And this testimony would not be complete without my Grace. We again were not prepared for our fourth child, but God needed her on this earth. When I got pregnant again after having three miscarriages and three very difficult pregnancies, I was scared. I was scared of the emotional roller coaster ride, and scared to begin to love another child growing inside me only to lose him or her. But I remember the Spirit taking me to the scripture found in Luke 1:38, *"Behold the maidservant of the Lord! Let it be to me according to your word."* That was my prayer that kept me surrendered to his will the entire pregnancy. Isabella Grace was born with no complications, and without me even having to push one moment. She literally came out on her own; a pure manifestation of grace in the flesh. Isabella loves to worship and continues to amaze me with her pure heart to love Jesus and others.

God did what He could only do to bring His seed, His weapon for the great spiritual war, into the earth through me. I am so thankful and honored to be entrusted with His seed on this earth. Each one of our children, are His children; His arrows and weapons.

The battle of the seed God has entrusted us with did not stop at birth – and nor will it for you. It doesn't take long for the world and our enemy to begin to influence them. In fact, did you know that by the time your child is six months old, they are already able to discern good and bad, right and wrong? Experts say that by the time a child is eight they have already developed their moral and spiritual compass, which will navigate them in all decisions.

The more I can share with you, trusting the Spirit of God is speaking through me, the more you are prepared for the battle, and will see victory. It is my heart to see victory for a generation of families. God Himself choose to use the language of warfare to describe parenting. I am simply going to use His very own perspective.

This chapter is dedicated to preparing you for the war, and equipping you in a greater capacity to see the seed of God entrusted to you manifest His glory on this earth. I am going to break down Psalm 127:3-6 through a prophetic look at how to be an excellent marksman with the arrow God has given you.

Weapon of Offense

Bow and arrows today are used more in sports than as weapon. But in Biblical times, they were used as one of the primary weapons of the day. Bow and arrows are an offensive weapon, best used to surprise your enemies. They are not good weapons to use when you're on the run. When a hunter today uses an arrow, his best shot is always going to be catching a deer, or whatever his prey is, by surprise while they are standing still. When a hunter or warrior is moving and trying to hit a target while being chased the accuracy goes way down.

Parenting was never supposed to be an army of believers that react out of defense; fighting on the run. Our King, the King of Heaven, intends for us to go and subdue the earth. That is an offense strategy.

Eye Dominance

Eye dominance is very important in being a marksman and shooting an arrow. What is your dominate eye in the Spirit as a Parent?

"Watch and pray, lest you enter into temptation. The spirit indeed is willing, but the flesh is weak." (Matthew 26:41).

If you are going to be a skilled marksman with your arrow placed in your hand, we must be diligent in seeing in the spirit and praying in a place of intercession against your enemy and his strategies. The best soldier is able to sleep with one eye open all the time. Look, watch, with your spiritual eyes, and see what's coming before it gets there.

Watch therefore, and pray always that you may be counted worthy to escape all these things that will come to pass, and to stand before the Son of Man." (Luke 21:36).

Praying always with all prayer and supplication in the Spirit, being watchful to this end with all perseverance and supplication for all the saints." (Ephesians 6:18).

The Spirit of God within us has eyes to see, He is a person and desires to give you His lenses to see through. To see both evil and good that surrounds you. To see inside the spirit realm where this war must be fought. Several of my favorite scriptures when it comes to spiritual warfare for our family are found in Nehemiah. Nehemiah has been given the task to lead the children of God to build the walls of the tabernacle back from destruction. Their enemy was real and was ready to hinder them on all sides. Nehemiah 4:9 says, *"Nevertheless we made our prayer to our God, and because of them we set a watch against them day and night."* Day and night they kept watch. We must be intentional, diligent, and vigilant in our watch for our family. As Nehemiah said, *"Do not be afraid of them. Remember the Lord, great and awesome, and fight for your brethren, your sons, your daughters, your wives, {our husbands}, and your houses." (Nehemiah 4:14).*

Hand Dominance

"But you, be strong and do not let your hands be weak, for your work shall be rewarded!" (2 Chronicles 15:7).

Parenting God's way is not easy, but we must not grow weary in the work we have set our hands to do. What should be our dominate hand as bows pulling back our arrows?

"You [God] have a mighty arm; Strong is Your hand, and high is Your right hand." (Psalm 89:13).

We should not trust in the strength of our own hands but in the strong right hand of the Lord to deliver our children to their attended target. In our own strength we will surely fail. In fact, have you ever tried to pull a bow back? If it is not calibrated to your own strength it is almost impossible to pull back. This does not mean you take your hands off, it simply means the Father's hands fold on top of yours and provides the power you need.

"And let us not grow weary while doing good, for in due season we shall reap if we do not lose heart." (Galatians 6:9).

Parenting God's way, disciplining your children in the spirit, is a sacrifice of worship in time and patience, but I promise you will reap what you sow.

Obtain Appropriate Gear

To avoid harming themselves all marksmen must wear protection gear. They wear arm guards, chest guards, finger guards.

"Therefore, take up the whole armor of God, that you may be able to withstand in the evil day, and having done all, to stand. Stand therefore, having girded your waist with truth, having put on the breastplate of righteousness, and having shod your feet with the preparation of the gospel of peace; above all, taking the shield of faith with which you will be able to quench all the fiery darts of the wicked one. And take the helmet of salvation, and the sword of the Spirit, which is the word of God." (Ephesians 6:13-17).

You must not go into battle without preparing yourself in your protective gear. It is imperative for the fight. I find it interesting that one of the places they would choose to wear the arrows is belted around their waist. Oh, that your child would be bound to you with the belt of truth! The truth of God connecting you, keeping you close, allowing for speed and quickness when using your arrow.

It is time to take our children into battle with us. Do not shut the door behind you, with all your protection gear on, with no weapon bound to you. Take them into the war. They need to see the enemy for themselves. And they need to see how you fight. They will catch what you did and start mimicking it.

Assume Correct Shooting Position

All marksman place their feet shoulder width apart firm. In proper form, the archer stands erect forming a T. Isn't that so interesting? We must learn that in battle we stand firm at the cross. Our victory is only absolute at the cross, there is no other way.

"Now therefore, stand and see this great thing which the LORD will do before your eyes." (1 Samuel 12:16).

We must learn to stand in the power of the cross and His resurrection and behold what the Lord will do through us.

"Have I not commanded you? Be strong and of good courage; do not be afraid, nor be dismayed, for the LORD your God is with you wherever you go." (Joshua 1:9).

Pick-Up Your Arrow

What we have done so far is all in anticipation of picking up your arrow. There is an element of trust and honor God has bestowed upon you; He has placed His greatest weapon of war in your quiver and ultimately trusting that you are going to take up your weapon and do something with it. Far too many parents within the body of Christ today delegate their God-given responsibility to raise their children up in the Lord on the church. Somehow, so many of us, even as God-fearing moms and dads who are warriors in the army of God, don't even pick up our greatest spiritual weapon and calling.

We feel that if we love our children, feed them, give them shelter, teach them good morals, take them to church, give them things, and give them a good scholastic education – somehow, we have done our job.

It is amazing to me how little our responsibility of giving our children a spiritual education passes through the mind of moms and dads. They do not understand the treasure and weapon God has put before them, and they never even pick up the calling. This, to me, is like being right in the middle of the war for your life and refusing to pick up the weapon handed to you to fight.

A weapon is only powerful and helpful in a fight if you pick it up. God has called us to step into our calling as the number one spiritual leader and minister to our children; *we can't afford not to do this*. There is a generation we can look to in the Bible that did not pick up their God given calling and weapon and the results were devastating for those parents.

Joshua 5 tells the story of God commanding Joshua to circumcise the children that came out of the wilderness. The reason told to us in Joshua 5:5-6 is, *"For all the people who came out [of Egypt] had been circumcised, but all the people born in the wilderness, on the way as they came out of Egypt, had not been circumcised. For the children of Israel walked forty years in the wilderness, till all the people who were men of war, who came out of Egypt, were consumed, because they did not obey the voice of the LORD."*

The men of war, those who were meant to expand God's kingdom and battle His enemies, died in the dry dead wilderness, never seeing the Promised Land because they failed to do as God had asked them to do; they failed to disciple, sanctify, set apart, prepare, and give their children over to the ways of God. They failed to pick up their calling and pick up their weapon and do what God commanded them to do with their seed. They neglected God's generational vision, and because of that, they died without ever seeing the promises of God fulfilled in their life.

God loves His children too much to watch them spiritually die in our hands; if we will not do it, He will find someone else who will. This, unfortunately, is why the church has had to step up to being more than a helpmate to parents; they have had to take on the calling of moms and dads because parents have neglected it.

I don't know about you, but I want to see the promises of God in my family in my lifetime. I want to be the one leading my children into the presence of God, teaching them the ways of God, and allowing my home to be a safe place to practice the gifts of God. I want to raise my children in a lifestyle of worship making my home a habitation place of his spirit. I want to teach my children to love God and others; to manifest His glory on the earth. I want to stand in the gate of my enemies and not be ashamed. I don't want anyone to take my place in the greatest calling of my life.

Aim

Here is our next challenge as warriors in this battle of the kingdoms for our family and seed. We must not just pick up our children, we must also decide to aim our weapon at its target.

Let's be honest, anyone can pick up a gun, but without proper aim it really is not going to help many in battle. A weapon is intended to be picked up and then aimed at its receiving target. What is our target?

"For we do not wrestle against flesh and blood, but against principalities, against powers, against the rulers of the darkness of this age, against spiritual hosts of wickedness in the heavenly places." (Ephesians 6:12).

Our enemy is never people, but always the Kingdom of darkness and His agendas.

"For this purpose the Son of God was manifested, that He might destroy the works of the devil." (1 John 3:8).

The target is always to destroy the works of the enemy. As Jesus was called to do, they are called to do the same. So how do we aim them at this target?

We shape them, cultivate them, and raise them, to counteract what the enemy is doing. To have an answer in this dark season that counteracts Satan and destroys his manipulation and lies – this is why the gifts of the Spirit in 1 Corinthians 12 where given to the church. It should look a bit like this when we aim them:

- "Ok, Satan. You want to bring diseases like cancer and MS? I am going to raise my children up to know that healing is the children's bread and it was done at the cross.
- "Satan, you want children to believe there is another gender than what God made them to be? I am going to raise my children to know that God knew all of humanity before they were in their mother's womb, and created them to be either male or female for a certain purpose in mind. But not only that, I am going to train them to speak, to prophesy, this truth into the ears of a generation that is walking in confusion."
- "Satan, you want to tear down the power of Christianity and raise up other gods? I am going to train my kids to walk in signs and wonders manifesting the power and love of Christ wherever they go, that all will know there is only one true God and that is Jesus Christ."
- "You want to kill unborn babies and sell their body parts as if they are more valuable dead than alive? I've got news

for you, Satan. I am going to aim my arrows right at our state houses, white house, and supreme courts."

- "I going to cultivate them to be world changes for the glory of God. I am going to make them a voice like a trumpet that will speak for the silenced children you have killed."

Where do you want to see your children go? What do you want to see them do?

Release

If we pick up our weapons, our children, and we aim them at their God-given target, but never release them to do it, nothing but frustration and failure will ever be produced from our efforts.

There is nothing more frustrating to someone than to be trained in a certain area, given a gift and ability to do something, only to never be able to do it. It's kind of like teaching a child how to ride a bike, but never allowing them to ride.

It is not just about preparing our children for their calling; it is about releasing them to do it. We must trust that what God has called them to do, and what He has equipped them to do through us, they are able to do it. We must learn to release them into ministry, not at some magical number of maturity we choose, but at the age they are now (barring your child is not an infant).

We are going to look at scripture to give us a better understanding of this. I am going to take you right to the family above all families in the Bible – Jesus and His Heavenly Father and earthly mother. I want to start by pointing out the release Jesus received from His Father on the day of His water baptism. Jesus had been discipled and prepared. His mother had taken up her weapon and calling and knew very much what her son was called to do; God had made sure of that. God Himself had aimed His son and poured into Him, filling Him with the Holy Spirit. Now, it was time for a release. As the dove, the Holy Spirit, came upon Jesus that day in the baptismal waters anointing Him for ministry, Jesus' father said, *"This is My beloved Son, in whom I am well pleased."* *(Matthew 3:17)*. These few words of affirmation released Jesus to do what He had been trained for…battle.

Our children are longing for us to affirm them into ministry.

They need to know we believe in them and are pleased with who they are in Christ. This kind of affirmation gives them the confidence to "do the stuff." But this is not where it ended with Jesus.

As in the order God established for a father and a mother to raise their children up in the Lord, Mary had her own moment of release. Many of us know the story well of Jesus's first miracle – turning the water into wine. It was noticed at the wedding that the wine had run out. Mary looked at her son and told Him the news. Jesus then replied to her, *"Woman, what does your concern have to do with Me? My hour has not yet come."* *(John 2:4)*. He knew exactly what Mary was saying between the lines – and all it took was one simple statement of release for Jesus to step into His calling. Mary said to the servants, *"Whatever He says to you, do it."* *(John 2:5)*. Jesus needed to hear from His mother that she believed in Him and had confidence He could do what He was called to do.

There is no age to the spirit, so as they grow and learn, give them a safe place within your home, in your neighborhood and community, to do that which they are called to do in the Lord. Let them know that they are weapons of God made for battle and then release them to do battle for Jesus!

Once that arrow leaves your bow, you must trust it will land exactly where you have aimed it. It may wobble and curve just a bit, but God will make their crooked path straight.

Train up a child in the way he should go, And when he is old he will not depart from it." (Proverbs 22:6).

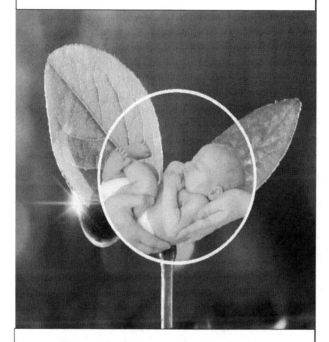

Chapter 4

Keeping the One thing, the One thing

This chapter I have devoted to bringing you prophetic insight and experiences that I have drawn from being a parent of children and family ministry over the years. It is a collection of modern day struggles and concerns I see happening within the families of the body that is enabling parents from keeping the One thing, the one thing in their home. What is the one thing?

"But seek first the kingdom of God and His righteousness, and all these things shall be added to you." (Matthew 6:33)

The one thing we must seek to have in our home, above all else, is the kingdom of God and His righteousness. Above all the noise of the culture around us, above all the day to day checklist and running from one thing to another, it is the Father's heart that our families seek His kingdom first. Everything else will flow out of that, if we allow it to.

Busyness is the Devils Playground

Some might think the statement, "busyness is the devil's playground," might sound again a bit dramatic and exaggerated, but in my opinion, busyness is the biggest stronghold in any given family of God today. Our culture has become so fast paced, so instantaneous for gratification, and "me" driven, that parents are often running in circles, never having time to make the ONE thing the ONE thing in their home.

I have always been so dumbfounded over the years of being a children and family minister, how we can park out our local school parking lots with parents who will go watch their child sing three songs with a group of a hundred other kids, never even really hearing their child's personal voice, but yet you can't get those same parents to invest in the spiritual education of their child. Scholastic education, without question, is important, and so is allowing your children to enjoy extracurricular activities and explore their gifts in life. But when it comes at the expense of teaching our children and giving the opportunity for spiritual education and gifts, we have missed the mark.

When I used to hold family gatherings for the city, I only had a handful of consistent families who would come to our monthly gatherings faithfully. They were the truly invested ones who made THE ONE, the ONE thing. Those same families were the ones whom I watch excel spiritually. Their children truly grew up loving Jesus and loving others. Their target was clear - the One thing.

Children's sports today have taken on a life of their own and consumes the family's time unlike anything else, especially if you have more than one child. I want you to know Jesus cares more about your family altar than about your child getting the participation trophy at soccer. Now does that mean we never let our kids do sports or recreational things? No, of course not. But it does mean that if you are not spending as much time seeking after Kingdom things with your family as you are everything else, you are not in line with God's word or heart for your family. We can't run around making sure our kids get to do the gymnastics, basketball, and soccer, and not make sure they get as much time to worship, learn about Jesus, and walk as light in the darkness.

In our family, if any sports or recreational activity interfered with Sunday's or midweek services it was off limits. It wasn't even a conversation or question. And as a family with four children, our rule was one sport per year per child. Today, parents spend more time running from one sport event to another, that they don't have time for Jesus themselves much less a family altar.

Time is a commodity. Wherever your heart is, is where you will invest your time. As your child gets older, especially as your family grows, it is important to stop every once in a while, and make sure what keeps your family's time... is not keeping you from the Kingdom. Don't be afraid to prune some things. I promise your kids will not look back as an adult and feel neglected because they could not join that competitive sports team. But, their heart and soul <u>will</u> suffer if you do not seek the Kingdom first and keep the ONE thing, the ONE thing. In fact, eternity just might be in the balance.

Guarding Technology

There is no question we live in a technology driven society. As a parent, it is a daunting task to keep up with all the new inventions of technology as they come out. This rat race of technology is fueled by world ideology or principles that do not line up with God's kingdom. Now does that means we throw the baby out with the bath water, and do not allow our family to engage in the technology culture? Does it mean it is all bad? No, of course not. The truth is there are a lot of good things about technology today. However, the reality is, the endless amount of technology at our fingertips has brought the "world" into our homes quicker than we can turn around. It is getting harder and harder each day to monitor what we see, hear, and read, for ourselves, much less our children.

Some might argue, as long as you know truth – what does it matter what you see, hear, or read? Our five senses have the power to alter our state of mind and change what we perceive as truth subconsciously. The more of the world your children are introduced to through social media and instant entertainment, the more power the world's systems and beliefs have to influence your child. As parents, we must be ready to fight and guard our children's innocence and belief systems.

For instance, did you know that according to many statistics out there, children are seeing and experiencing their first pornography picture and video and age 8? Now, you might find that hard to believe, but this is absolutely true and going on today. I will share that our own family has battled with this spirit. Our son Samuel, our oldest I have already spoken about, began to struggle with a pornography addiction starting in the sixth grade; he would have been maybe eleven. We were unaware for several years about it because he had open access to the internet on our family computer. The addiction continued to grow stronger in his life when he received his first phone and could use the internet freely from the privacy of his room. It enslaved him for years, and Satan used it as a way to gain access into his life and try to destroy his calling and purposes. Today, many kids receive their first phone by the time they are in elementary school. It is impossible to know what demonic influences are out there, popping up on your child's phone.

Now, I couldn't possibly give you advice in this book on every social media account and technology device out there. They would change before this book got published! To be honest, I thank God I have a husband who knows so much more about technology than I do. He has been able to make informed decisions about guarding our children with technology far more than I could ever. But I will share a few things we have guarded to just get you started. After we found out about our son's addiction, we placed software on our computer that locked up unsafe and inappropriate websites. This is something that is done at businesses and schools. Again, once your children are given their first phone, this becomes much more difficult. You can, however, lock up the internet on their phones, as well as their other devices, and/or control how long and what time they can use it. We also did not allow are children to have their devices in their room at bedtime. We realized they were staying up until the middle of night talking to friends and interacting on social media.

Speaking of social media. We did not allow our children to get on any social media account until they were 13. Even then, it was limited, and we had to be one of their friends. We also required them to share all of their passwords with us and at any time we had the right to get their device and check out their activity and messages.

This may seem harsh and over-controlling, but times have changed my friend. This is not the same world your mother or grandmother were raised up in. If my son was here to add to his testimony he would tell you the living hell he went through with a pornography addiction. All it takes is one glance, one friend who they trust, one advertisement, one dare. Kids also compare themselves to each other using social media. It is a fake front that brings a fake reality – to a peer pressured generation. All Satan needs, is one little lie to stick, and he has a door to destroy truth in your child.

Breaking the Silence

This actually brings me to one other huge issue with technology and our children. Several years ago, the Holy Spirit begin to speak a word to me about this generation. He told me, "A generation who has endless ways to communicate has lost the art of communication." He went on to take me through all the ways kids today communicate. They mostly text, message, send emoji's, but rarely do they ever pick up a phone and talk or even talk face to face. You get a bunch of kids in a room with technology and they will text each other instead of raising their heads up, looking each other in the eye, and speaking.

The consequences of a generation who do not know how to use their voice has been absolutely detrimental. In a generation that will be tagged as the communication generation of the 21st century, they may very well be the most silent generation of modern day history. Of all the endless ways this generation has to communicate, not one way requires them to open their mouth and speak. In this generation filled with lips not moving and ears not hearing, allowing modern day technology to deceive them into thinking that their voice is being heard, silence has fallen on the land. In this modern day generation where playing video games, texting, instant messaging, and Facebook is the norm, the sound and voice of heaven has been silenced, held captive to the cultures ideologies of what they must do to keep up with success in this world. I believe as wonderful as modern day technology is, Satan has strategized to use it to silence a generation.

Why would Satan ever try to strategize to silence a generation? There is nothing more powerful than the spoken word for a believer. God Himself created nothing in this world without it being spoken into existence first; God said and it was. He has created all of us in His image, and according to scripture, Life and Death is in the power of our tongue (Proverbs 18:21).

We see just how much power God has placed in our tongues in the story of Moses and the rock. In Numbers 20, we see a very familiar story unfold after the children of God had been in the wilderness for about a month. They began to complain to Moses about their lack of water. They became very angry that God had delivered them out of slavery only to seemingly allow them to die of thirst in the wilderness. Moses and Aaron went to lie on their faces before God crying out for Him to do something. I am sure their prayers were of desperation; fearing the people of God may retaliate against them.

God did answer them that day and gave them these instructions, *"Take the rod; you and your brother Aaron gather the congregation together. Speak to the rock before their eyes, and it will yield its water; thus you shall bring water for them out of the rock, and give drink to the congregation and their animals."* (Numbers 20:8). They cried out for direction and instruction and God answered them.

Now you would think Moses, in his desperation crying out to God, would immediately go and do what God told him to do. No. Moses went to the people and said to them, *"Hear now, you rebels! Must we bring water for you out of this rock? Then Moses lifted his hand and struck the rock twice with his rod; and water came out abundantly, and the congregation and their animals drank." (Numbers 20:10-11).* The passage goes on to say that because of Moses' unbelief he would not be allowed to enter the Promised Land.

Moses wasn't forbidden to go into the Promised Land because He disobeyed God. However, the *root* of his disobedience was a lack of belief. Moses was not allowed to go into the Promised Land because he did not believe in the power of his words (or rather, God's words through him), to bring life out of something that was dead. From the time of the burning bush, Moses constantly struggled with the idea that He could be used of God to speak with power and authority – that his words mattered. God was offering Moses an unbelievable opportunity to partner with Him to create life. The dead, dry, dirty rock in the wilderness had no power in itself to spew living water out from it, but God's creative, powerful, and living words through Moses *had* what it took. Yet, Moses *struck* the rock instead of *speaking* to it. He lashed out in anger at the people calling them rebels as he hit the rock. Despite hearing from God and knowing what to do, Moses used his *own* strength and flesh instead of trusting in the Spirit of God upon Him, and His voice, to bring life. If he had used his voice that day, he would have gotten to place his feet on the Promised Land.

In the days of Samuel, God found a voice He could use to speak His Word through. But, it wasn't the person you would expect. It was a child; a boy called Samuel. The scriptures say that the Word of the Lord was rare, and there was no widespread revelation in the days of Samuel (1 Samuel 3:1). It was in that silence, that the Lord chose a young boy to become both a prophet and a priest unto Him. In the silence, God chose the young to confound the old and the wise, and speak His word through prophecy.

Your child could be just that voice. It is time to break the silence. Teach them how to speak and use their voice, teach them how to declare the Word. And, for heaven's sake – teach them how to communicate with others around them using their voice! There is something about the voice that brings communication and personalization. I believe technology has stripped a generation of not just thier voice, but of relationship with each other. Fight against the hand of the enemy who will try to muffle the voice of your children and family.

Identity Crisis

Today, in many of our churches we have heard the term "identity crisis." What does that mean exactly? Many equate it to the homosexual and transgender confusion going on today. But in actuality, it goes far deeper than that. Those issues are simply one way the deeper crisis of identity is manifesting.

The root of all identity crises is found in a Fatherless generation. When I am speaking of a "Fatherless generation," I am not speaking of the broken homes of society where kids are without natural fathers. That again is only a manifestation of the deeper root in the spirit. I am talking about a saturation of a culture who does not know their heavenly Father, and as a result cannot receive, walk in, or understand their place as a child of God.

This Fatherless spirit is as much in the church as in the world. Speaking to you from a children and family minister perspective, I have seen firsthand our failed attempts to raise a generation up who walk in the confidence of being a son or daughter of the Father. More times than not, we introduce children, or adults for that matter, to Jesus our Savior and God our Creator. We hand them a lens of Christianity to look through that separates them from being a part of a family. We teach them they need to be saved, forgiven of their sins, so that they may have eternal life. We teach them that God was their Creator and all powerful one, but we don't go beyond that. Yet, Jesus died on the cross for far greater things than to be our Savior. He sacrificed His life so we could be brought back to the Father.

"Now all things are of God, who has reconciled us to Himself through Jesus Christ, and has given us the ministry of reconciliation." (2 Corinthians 5:18).

Sin separated us from the Father, and through Christ, we are to find our place back in His arms; our identity is found in Him. We are His DNA. We are His beloved. God's heart is clear, *"I will be a Father to you, And you shall be My sons and daughters, Says the LORD Almighty." (2 Corinthians 6:18).*

Children and adults who don't lay hold of this revelation or are never introduced to it, innately seek out acceptance in all the wrong places. They search the world over to find their place; to find where they belong. We have so neglected to introduce a generation of believers to sonship, they are lost in who they are and who He is in them. An identity crisis for sure.

In fact, I will go further to say I have seen the spirit of fear sweep over the church from children to adults. This is again, I believe, is simply a manifestation of the identity crisis.

"For you did not receive the spirit of bondage again to fear, but you received the Spirit of adoption by whom we cry out, "Abba, Father." (Romans 8:15).

The Spirit of fear enslaves and blinds children of God to not be able to see who they are in the Father. When you can teach your child to know who lives in them and who they belong to, they are empowered to walk in boldness and freedom; confident that they are a son or daughter of the Living God. He is truly a good Father and your child needs to know that, be constantly reminded of that, and experience the Fathers love daily.

"Fear not, for I have redeemed you; I have called you by your name; You are Mine." (Isaiah 43:1).

Knowing someone comes by experience. We can teach our children to know about the Father, never leading them to know the Father. They need His presence in their life. Jesus said, *"Let the little children come to Me, and do not forbid them; for of such is the kingdom of heaven." (Matthew 19:14).* Jesus didn't say tell them about me; He said bring them to me. They are mine. I want them to know Me intimately; to touch Me and feel Me. Religion will bring to your child all kinds of manifestations of identity crises. Relationship will bring the Father's love and confidence to be who they were created to be.

Seeing the Forest Above the Tree Line

It is important that you, as a family, keep the bigger picture in mind. We have discussed briefly God's purpose for earth and humanity. He created His children to fill the earth with His kingdom. Each one of us is His seed filled with purpose and callings He has planned for us. He called us to manifest His glory on this earth.

His plans for us to do just that are found in *Matthew 5:13-16, "You are the salt of the earth; but if the salt loses its flavor, how shall it be seasoned? It is then good for nothing but to be thrown out and trampled underfoot by men. You are the light of the world. A city that is set on a hill cannot be hidden. Nor do they light a lamp and put it under a basket, but on a lampstand, and it gives light to all who are in the house. Let your light so shine before men, that they may see your good works and glorify your Father in heaven.*

Life gets chaotic in a family; taking the kids to school, going to work, church, practices, cooking dinner, laundry, and some time is in there for finding time to sleep and clean the house. We try to find some sense of a routine to keep ourselves from going crazy. But the concern I see, in some ways, is we can't see the forest above the tree line. It is important that you, as a family, find some way to fulfill God's ultimate call to be the salt and light to a dark world. Many serve within their church and that is great and should be done. But ultimately, you are the church at home and in your neighborhood and community.

Our walk as Christians should not begin at the door of the church and stop at the grocery store, neighborhood, or within our day to day living and going. Your child needs to grow up within the concept that they were placed here to shift atmospheres and bring the Kingdom to earth. Through their good works, the Father will be glorified, and the Kingdom will come.

Most would think of good works as serving the needy, being kind to everyone, demonstrating the fruits of the Spirit. These things are absolutely a portion of good works. But even the lost can serve the needy. Jesus Himself is our model. Jesus did not neglect serving the poor and needy. He feed those who were hungry and gave drink to those who were thirsty. But He did so much more than that.

"The Spirit of the LORD is upon Me, Because He has anointed Me To preach the gospel to the poor; He has sent Me to heal the brokenhearted, To proclaim liberty to the captives And recovery of sight to the blind, To set at liberty those who are oppressed; To proclaim the acceptable year of the LORD." (LUKE 4:18-19).

Jesus' assignment, that has now become our assignment, is to bring the Kingdom to earth. God has given us His spirit, His power, to use the nine gifts of the Spirit (1 Corinthians 12:1-11) and destroy the works of the devil. Teach them how to lay hands on the sick, teach them how to prophecy, teach them how to discern spirits, teach them how to have wisdom. Then, go model before them how to use those gifts in the marketplace to bring God's Kingdom to earth. Good works is not what we can do – there is only One who is good and that is the Father. Good works is what He can do through us. It's the supernatural that glorifies the Father.

One of my favorite ways to do this kind of activation is through a method known as "Treasure Hunting." The treasure is people you run across in your day to day lives that you may have never met before. The idea is for you to either intentionally or as you go, pray for God to give you a treasure that day; someone who He wants to speak to. Listen for Him to speak to you and give you hints about who the person is you are to approach (i.e. maybe what they are wearing, what they look like, where you might find them). If you find someone with those clues, approach them in the way you desire. Ask them concerning prayer or about anything God lays on your heart about them. This is a perfect activity to do as a family. Let your kids see you do it, then give them a turn to do it. You will not be perfect, you will have a laugh or two over mistakes, but I promise – God will show up. He always does. This will model before your children how to walk out their Christ walk in a way that fulfills the heart of the Father. Jesus was about His Father's business – we should be too.

Parent Dedication

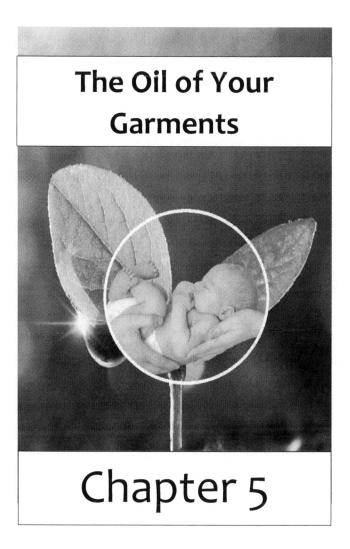

The Oil of Your Garments

Chapter 5

Family Priesthood

What I have learned along the way of ministering to parents, and through my own personal experience, is that where we are spiritually as parents, directly affects our kid's spiritual life. This is not by accident but by divine order of God.

Let me take you right to scripture and build a foundation for what I will be discussing in this chapter.

"And you shall bring his sons and clothe them with tunics. You shall anoint them, as you anointed their father, that they may minister to Me as priests; for their anointing shall surely be an everlasting priesthood throughout their generations." (Exodus 40:14-15).

In this scripture, God is establishing the earthly priesthood through Aaron and his sons. Notice that as Aaron was anointed and robed with priestly garments, so were his sons. This is the very first time we can actually see an order of family ministry mapped out in scripture.

The priesthood was established to be a family ministry; one generation to another, creating a perpetual lifestyle of worship before God. It is the original command of God in the garden, to subdue the earth and multiply, manifested through the entity of the family.

Colossians 2:17 and Hebrews 8:5 tells us that the tabernacle and the laws of which to worship within, was a copy and shadow of the original in heaven. Although Jesus fulfilled the law and the acts of worship in the Old Testament making them not necessary today, the principles and foreshadowing still apply to us as New Testament believers.

In fact, Jesus makes it clear in 1 Peter 2:5 that we are to continue the role of the priesthood; *"You also, as living stones, are being built up a spiritual house, a holy priesthood, to offer up spiritual sacrifices acceptable to God through Jesus Christ."*

God's thoughts and motives reached far beyond one man named Aaron. They reached into the depths of eternity and established the ancient paths of His Holy priesthood, those who would serve and worship Him all the days of their lives. When we accept the commission of 1 Peter 2:5, to become a Holy Priest unto the Lord, we must also accept the commission of family ministry. What God has established he will never hinder; His word and ways are the same yesterday, today, and forever.

We must get beyond the "me," and get to the "we," and take our children by the hand and teach them how to worship and serve the Lord. God knew that in order to keep a Holy line of priests, the family must worship and serve Him together. This is why He called parents to be the primary spiritual leader and teacher of their children. If there becomes a gap or void between the spirituality of parents and children, God has lost a generation. I believe this is where we are today. Families are so far separated spiritually; husbands and wives, sons and daughters, that Satan has free reign and an open door to do as he pleases.

Spiritual Unity

The anointing of Aaron and His priestly robe was not just for Him, it ran down his head and his garments to his children.

"Behold, how good and how pleasant it is for brethren to dwell together in unity! It is like the precious oil upon the head, running down on the beard, the beard of Aaron, Running down on the edge of his garments." (Psalm 133:1-2).

Many have drawn this analogy to the church, but as we now know through the model of the Priesthood, this scripture speaks more about unity of the home than anywhere.

The oil that runs down our head and garments as priest of our homes, directly affects the anointing oil of our children. When there is no spiritual unity in the home, disorder and chaos rules over our family. Sometimes the discord is with a husband or wife (or ex-spouse) that are non-believers. This makes unity extremely difficult and almost impossible. But sometimes we must look at the oil of our own garments as parents and make sure what we are passing down to our children is holy and of God.

Tainted Oil

I want to begin with a caution about Tainted Oil: mixing the anointing God has given us, His oil, with that of the worlds. I have previously already talked about some of my concerns of compromise in the home, so I will not go into this in depth. But it is worth mentioning here that we must take the time to evaluate our oil as priests and make sure we are keeping ourselves sanctified as the priests were required to do —not out of a religious mindset, but out of a love of the Father. A holy reverence to the relationship we have with Him should compel us to desire to please Him in all things. To keep our walk guarded and our eyes clean.

The priest, according to God's statue and laws, had to keep themselves sanctified and set a part for the work of ministry.

This would ensure that their anointing would not be tainted and it would ensure that a Godly and Holy lineage of Priests would be passed down from generation to generation. This was exactly why Eli and his sons were kicked out of the priesthood. We must think about how our actions affect our children.

God has anointed us as parents so that our anointed oil runs down our robe to our children's, we must be careful not to be the hand that contaminates the anointing they receive. Many parents are walking in and doing works of unrighteousness and are still expecting the oil of their garments to be holy and uncontaminated.

Enough Oil

Ok, we are going to switch gears a little now from making sure your oil is not tainted to asking yourselves this question: Do you have enough oil? You cannot give what you have not received or have to give.

I think this principle is most trying for parents. The question may not be tainted oil, but oil at all. We tend to give, give, give, and never seem to have the time to receive. But the principal remains the same; we cannot give what we have not received. We want to be some kind of supermom or dad, who has it all together. We want so desperately have all the creative ideas, and see God use our kids in supernatural ways. We want to teach them and train them how to walk in the Spirit, to use the gifts of the spirit, how to heal the sick, prophesy to their generation, teach them how to be authentic worshipers with a heart for God's presence, teach them to know the word of God, to be prayer warriors, and world changers.

But the question is...are WE all those things? Are we making sure we have what it takes to give? Do we have the oil from walking in the presence, love, and obedience of the Father and doing His work on earth ourselves? Or are we trying to give something we don't?

As we pour out unto our children, all too often, we don't see the results we want to see so we think the answer is to pour out more, pour out more, until we fall down in sheer exhaustion. But the problem may be that we have not kept our lamps, our garments – our temple – full of the oil of God. What is running down from our garments, then, is flesh, and not oil at all. I can tell you from experience this happens more times than we think.

"Seek first the kingdom of God and His righteousness, and all these things shall be added to you." (Matthew 6:33).

God never intended for us to become superheroes – that is an honor for him and him alone. What He does desire us to be as parents – is to be Priests anointed with oil from His kingdom. He desires us to be kingdom carriers; to seek Him and His kingdom first, and out of that overflow of His kingdom we pour out.

The kingdom of Heaven is the very power, authority, righteousness, and justice of the King Himself; heaven on earth. How often do we seek after the Kingdom of heaven first?

"When the Spirit of truth comes, he will guide you into all the truth, for he will not speak on his own authority, but whatever he hears he will speak, and he will declare to you the things that are to come. He will glorify me, for he will take what is mine and declare it to you. All that the Father has is mine; therefore I said that he will take what is mine and declare it to you." (John 16:12-15).

Jesus said one of the roles of the Holy Spirit is to give us all things of the Father. We have all of heaven at our disposal. That means we don't have to ever give of ourselves, but instead give out of the overflow of heavens oil. A good test if we are giving out of the overflow of anointing is if we are weary and exhausted.

As a parent the demand on your calling is heavy, exhausting, and eternally impactful making the pressure overwhelming sometimes.

But it doesn't have to be that away, or at least continually.

"Come to me, all you who are weary and burdened, and I will give

you rest. Take my yoke upon you and learn from me, for I am gentle and humble in heart, and you will find rest for your souls. For my yoke is easy and my burden is light (Matthew 11:30)."

Don't Work for God, Work with God

A yoke is a large piece of wood that would be strapped around a working animal so that its master could lead it around. It is time to be yoked up to Christ our Master. Learn to be in constant partnership and fellowship with what God wants to do through and with you. We talked about this briefly as we learned to use our arrows.

It may look the same as other parents; it may look different. Don't compare yourself with others, but be confident and who you are yoked up with; that is Christ. As the animals had to listen to instructions and guidance from their master, we do too. Listen for His voice daily. Follow the footsteps of daddy God and be attentive of pouring out only want he desires you to. Jesus never did anything that he did not see or hear His father doing. Don't give in to culture pressure or even church pressure to be all and do all. If we seek to work with God, we will find he gives us what we need to pour out and then more. His grace is sufficient to empower us to do what we cannot do on our own. We are never lacking when we are yoked up with Christ because He is our source.

Find Yourself Daily inside of Christ

Another word we can use for being yoked up is to abide.

"I am the true vine, and My Father is the vinedresser. Every branch in Me that does not bear fruit He takes away; and every branch that bears fruit He prunes, that it may bear more fruit. You are already clean because of the word which I have spoken to you. Abide in Me, and I in you. As the branch cannot bear fruit of

itself, unless it abides in the vine, neither can you, unless you abide in Me." (John 15:1-4).

You want to see the fruit of your womb bear fruit, abide inside of Christ. We live in a society that is about giving our kids what they call a "well-rounded" childhood. God never called us to be balanced in life; a little bit of this a little bit of that. We were called to go after and obtain all of heaven and bring it to earth. Don't concern yourself with giving your children a balanced childhood with soccer practices, basketball practices, music lessons, girl scouts, after school scholastics, and all and everything you can fit into a day and week. Be only interested in giving them one thing; and that one thing is Jesus, everything else will be added to it!

If you have to prune some things away in your life so you can make time to abide with Christ, do it! That is not selfishness that is Godly wisdom.

Be Content with Each Season

I believe some of our striving and frustration as parents comes from not being content. We can't wait until they can crawl, then walks, then talk, go to school; we are looking always forward never in the present and content.

Again, in Matthew 11:30 Jesus says, "learn from me." Jesus was content with each season of His life. I oftentimes think of what it must have been like for Jesus as a boy, teenager, and young man all the way up until he hit 30. He knew he was called for greater things. He was fully God and man. He must have, at times, been itching to get out there and do the stuff. What about his parents? They must have wanted to see Jesus do what He was born to do as soon as could talk and walk.

There is a season for everything as a parent. I remember

wondering if the sleepless nights would ever end. I remember wondering if I would ever feel "normal" again. I remember wondering if I would ever be able to do anything else but change diapers, cook dinner, and give baths.

But the time and season came where the bottle feeding ended, the diaper changing ended, the baths ended, the homework ended, and even sadly, having six people at my dinner table ended. But to every time there is a season (Ecclesiastes 3).

Find Jesus in the Moment

Part of being content is to find Jesus right where you are. He knows where you are and realizes that maybe you don't have but 1 or 2 minutes to be with Him; His grace is sufficient.

Think about this: Jesus never stopped abiding with the Father or being God when he was playing in the backyard or going to school. We are called to be the Tabernacle of God. That does not stop because we have to wash dishes or go to work. Find your Selah Moment.

Not every season, not every day is going to be about signs, miracles, and wonders; Jesus was even content in the season of death. Now that is a hard pill to swallow. But we all must go through death before resurrection life can come. Find yourself seeking the Kingdom, even in the moments of death and trails. Don't fight the process, just seek the Kingdom, and you will find even in your death you will have oil on your garments. Wasn't that the case with Jesus? Remember the story of Mary anointing him right before his death? I find that in the season of my worst horrific personal fires, God gives me the most revelation and anointing.

Family Altar

I want to encourage you to use the model the Father gave us right in the scriptures for family ministry. We have briefly addressed the priestly model. Aaron and sons, father and son, served and worshiped God together at the altar. The altar of God was essentially created to be a family altar. One generation to another learning how to serve and worship God 24/7; a culture and lifestyle of worship. This is God's heart for you as a family. To pass down God's legacy and inheritance to the next generation at your own family altar. In fact, I believe He cares more about you establishing a family altar at home, far more than He does you making sure you get your child to church.

Now I am certainly not saying to not go to church, or it get them involved in the children's ministry of your church. Church is Biblical, a great helpmate for families, and an excellent way for your child to build relationships and friendships that are healthy and godly. But God has not called you to take your children to children's ministry, He has called your take ministry to your children. God designed family ministry to start in the home.

Years ago, the Lord led me to start hosting family gatherings for my local city. We ran them for six years. During this time, He began to unfold for me a pattern of family ministry modeled after the Tabernacle of Moses – a creative and Biblical approach to engaging the entire family in acts of worship right in your home. A pattern of family ministry that goes far beyond a family devotional, but uses the postures of worship in the Tabernacle, and their New Testament reflections, to bring relevant, presence-driven, intentional, and engaging worship to your entire family. Several years ago, I wrote a book for parents that outlined a step-by-step approach to this approach to the family altar. It is called **Creating a Family Altar**. You can purchase this resource from our ministry website or Amazon.

I encourage you to begin this paradigm of worship with even just your spouse, if your child is an infant. As you make this a common activity in your home, your child will see it as natural and normal too. As they become toddlers and elementary age, they can begin to participate more and more. There is nothing that will build spiritual unity and love in a home, more than family worship.

I want to share one simple family act of worship with you among so many I can share. It is family communion. Family communion is a worship posture found in the Outer Court of the Tabernacle at the Altar of Sacrifice. It is an easy and engaging way Jesus created for us all to commune and connect with Him at the altar. Communion as a family does not have to be as formal as church communion is. You can use elements as simple as bread and any kind of juice or drink. The most important thing is bringing your family together to focus on what Jesus accomplished at the cross.

It is important when doing family worship that you get your entire family to engage (of course with the exception of small children). Most children can start engaging, in some way, three years and up. Most children, starting at six years of age, can fully engage. In regards to communion, I encourage you to each share in reading from 1 Corinthians 11:17-23. Have someone as well pray over the bread and juice. You could even focus on healing at this time and pray for anyone who is sick. My family uses spiritual holidays like Easter, Thanksgiving, and Christmas to engage in family communion as well.

Birthdays are a built-in opportunity to create a family altar moment. In our family, the evening of a family member's birthday, we all lay hands on them and pray blessings over their next year of life. Our **Stone Moments Manual** for parents, as I previous mentioned, has 72 family acts of worship at the family altar. It is a great resource to have. I have given you a list of all our great resources for parents in the back of this book. You can find them on our website and at Amazon.com.

My Prayer for You

My heavenly Father, I thank you for every mother and father of God you have somehow led to read this book. I pray now that every word that was eternal and life-giving would go forth and bring your fruit to their families. I pray you will give them Godly wisdom, understanding, and anointing beyond their natural capacity to raise, nurture, and teach your children, your seed, how to love you and love others. I pray that they would arise, take up their greatest calling, and do the work of ministry as parents of the Most High. Keep them under your blood as warriors on the front lines that they may learn to use your weapon of choice, destroying the works of the devil in this day and hour. May the fullness of your glory come through each child till your Kingdom covers the earth, one seed at a time.

In Jesus Name, Amen.

About the Author

I wanted to start off by sharing a bit about my own testimony as a parent. Even though I was raised up around the church and the things of God, due to the tragic loss of my own father at four years old, my family life became broken. My mother, who I love and respect dearly, at the time, was a young twenty seven year old widow with two little girls; my sister being six, and me four. She did the best with what she knew how to do, but unfortunately it lead us down the road of living a much separate family life than what we knew in church. Today my mother and step Father love the Lord very much and I could not be prouder of them.

Even despite the culture and family life I was raised in that was confusing and compromising, as I child, I knew my Daddy God was there and I had conversations with Him frequently. I stayed close to Him until I hit my teen years. But without the foundations of a Christian home life to stand on, I drifted away from the Lord for eight years. During that time away from the Lord I met my high school sweetheart, Jason, who did not know the Lord at all. We married and began to start a life with each other.

Neither I nor my husband walked with the Lord as we started our family. But God was soon to change that. When our first child, our only son, was two, I found myself struggling with keeping a viable pregnancy. After my second miscarriage, I was desperate for God's love and presence again and returned back to him. Within the first couple of months of finding a church and relationship with Jesus again, I got pregnant for the third time since our son was born. And again an early ultrasound detected that I was going to lose this child too. With the flu and a 104 temperature, our newly found pastor came over and prayed for me. The next week another ultrasound testified to a miracle of a healthy little girl we soon named Faithanna. Our season of emotional trauma was not yet over though. Faithanna was born with a kidney disease that took one of her kidneys from her. Eight months after having Faithanna I then got pregnant with twins, one of which I lost. The precious little girl that survived we named Hope. And to add to the top of this incredible time of trials and tribulations, Jason got laid off from his job during 911 and was unemployed for eighteen months.

The revelation that came out of that incredible time of battle though is what made us into the parents we are today. Jason received Christ while I was pregnant with Faithanna, and as we together, began to walk down the road that was set before us, we realized that God was doing something incredible in us every step of the way. We found ourselves with a deep revelation that having children is a miracle and a precious gift from God not to be taken for granted. There was a deep knowing in our Spirit that God had chosen us to be the parents of our children, and that He was beckoning us to be a part of something bigger than ourselves in this role. We knew that if we desired for our family to take a different path then perhaps our childhoods had taken us, it would require from us radical change and intentional effort.

We began to evaluate what we desired for our children and for our family; what things mattered the most at the end of the day. We set out to do things differently, but most importantly Biblically. God wasn't just going to be a part of our family life, but our life. As we fell madly in the love with God and His presence, and made that our lifestyle, our children naturally followed. We didn't have to force them or even entice them. Just as Jesus saw and did what His Father was doing, they saw what daddy (and mommy) did and that became the normal culture for them. The family altar was established in our family by creating a lifestyle of His presence.

The Lord eventually gifted us with one more child, who I affectionately call my "grace" child because I had no complication carrying her whatsoever. Her name is Isabella Grace. As I finish writing this book we are preparing to send out our first and only son off to college to study ministry. Our three girls underneath him are fourteen, thirteen, and six. I can say, only by the grace of God and our willingness to intentionally go after His presence in our family, they all don't just love the Lord but are passionately pursing Him in a lifestyle of worship. Their hearts are not intertwined with the world, but it is clear what they make their life and priority; God's presence and will in every way.

Through the years, the Lord has used us to share His heart for His children and families in both Children's Ministry and Youth Ministry, and now through our own family ministry called Chosen Stones. I am also currently the Ohio Director for Kids in Ministry int., which is foundered and directed by Becky Fischer in North Dakota. I am honored and excited with anticipation to partner with God to see a whole generation of families bring the altar back into their homes, causing authentic transformation in their families, in our churches, and the culture around us.

About Our Ministry

Chosen Stones Ministries is a focused spirit lead and spirit empowered ministry to families; teaching families how to live and walk by the spirit of God and how to worship in spirit and in truth making worship a lifestyle not a place they go.

We host monthly presence-driven family worship gatherings that engage all ages of the family young and old alike. In these gatherings we train families how to worship together and make a habituation place for the Holy Spirit through modeling and facilitating what we call "acts of Worship". These acts of worship often time use object lessons like communion, laying on of hands, studying and discussing scripture, praying scripture, listening for the voice of God, and using the gifts of the Spirit, all within the paradigm of the family.

It is our desire that the church at large grab hold of our vision for families and begin to host their own presence-driven family worship gatherings. As we equip the families of God to live a lifestyle of worship and create an altar for His presence within their home, our churches will become stronger, more spiritually mature, and filled with the presence of God. It starts in the home!

I currently write presence driven family devotionals for families, host yearly training conferences that include parents, and accept invitations to come to churches to train leaders and parents, and host family conferences.

Alicia White, founder and Director of Chosen Stones Ministries

www.chosenstones.org, more information: info@chosenstones.org

Family Resources Recommended

Creating A Family Altar

I highly recommended purchasing this resource for your families within your church to read as you begin to birth presence-driven family ministry. This will help them grab hold of the vision for their families and inspire them to engage in your ministry and in home family worship.

Stone Moments Family Manual

Although written for families, I highly recommended purchasing this resource as you begin hosting family gatherings. It has 72 creative spirit lead acts of worship you can do with your families.

Act of Worship

This resource although written as a church curriculum, is an excellent resource for home. All 52 acts of worship in this curriculum are in the Stone Moments Manual but in this resource each one comes with a full

Radical Worship Family Devotional

Your families will go on a 52 day journey of worship from before the earth was created, to the Garden of Eden, through the Tabernacle of Moses, to the Garden of Gethsemane with Jesus, right to Mary's alabaster box. The Tabernacle teaching in this book came straight out of the pages of this devotional to be shared as a family with discussion questions and presence-driven family worship exercises.

Living Stones Family Devotional

Through a detailed word study of how God has chosen to use stones in the "seen" world, a picture begins to form that reveals who we are as living stones in the "unseen" world according to 1 Peter 2:4. Your family will take a 40 day journey from the Old Testament to the New, discovering mysteries hidden in God's word to find your calling as Living Stones. This devotional is filled with creative spirit lead worship activities that go along with each subject

Kingdom Family Devotional

This resource is full of 84 days your families can experience learning about our King and the Kingdom of Heaven together. Through the view finder of a kingdom, they will discover their own purpose for being born on this earth and feel a since of belonging to something greater than themselves. Spirit filled acts of worship is all included in this resources for your families

Amazing Grace Family Devotional

This 52 day devotional is all about helping your families find Biblical authentic grace. This resource brings a holistic view of grace that encompasses a foundation of grace based upon a biblical perspective of who God is, who we are not, why we need grace through Christ, the right posture to receive grace, and what the work of grace produces in every believer and family that is yielded to the Holy Spirit. There are opportunities given for presence-driven family worship in the devotional as well.

Malachi Movement Parent's Small Group Course

In this eight week small group course, parents will be invited into a Selah moment with Jesus; a pause in all the madness of family life to find God's heart for them as parents for such a time as this. Using the Tabernacle of Moses, a set-by-step blueprint on how to practically apply God's heart and vision in their family will unfold, reestablishing the family altar and cultivating the atmosphere of the presence of God inside their home. A facilitator manual will lead parents in a time of teaching using our session introduction videos and notes provided in this manual. Along with the Facilitator Manual, there is a Parent's Workbook. The workbook provides notes for each session, a Malachi Moment family worship time for the home, and journal pages to pen what God speaks to them through the lesson and family Malachi Moments.

34875492R00046

Made in the USA
Middletown, DE
30 January 2019